cat (kat), *n.* [*pl.* CATS (kats) AS. *catte*, akin to G. *katze* < LL. *cattus*, etc., all via Celt.; prob. IE. base **qat-*, to bear young, seen in L. *catulus*. 1. a small, lithe, soft-furred animal, domesticated since ancient times, and often kept as a pet or for killing mice. 2. . . .

By B. Kliban ‎ ‎ WP Workman Publishing Co. New York

ISBN: 0-911104-54-2 (paper)

ISBN: 0-911104-87-9 (cloth)

Design by Paul Hanson

Manufactured in the United States of America

Workman Publishing Company
231 East 51st Street
New York, New York 10022

First cloth edition September 1976
            2   4   6   8   7   5   3

To Norton, Nitty and their mother Noko Marie the Snake, and Burton Rustle, formerly unrelated but now family.

How to draw a Qat

HERE'S WHAT YOU'LL NEED!

CIRCLES

DARK

DOTS

STRAIGHT LINES

QAT EYES

CURVED LINES

STRIPES

TRIANGLE

1. 2. 3. 4. 5. 6.

GRAND CHAMPION
Burton Rustle

Tiny Cat & Fountain Pen

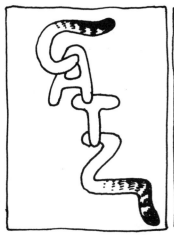

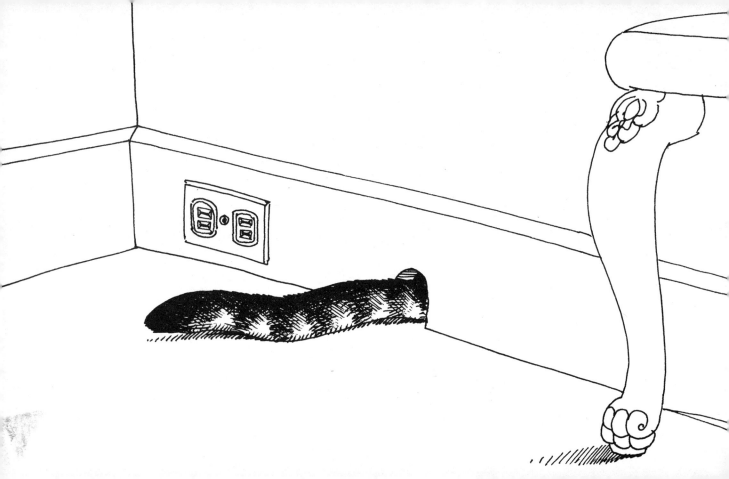

Burton Nov 72

How to draw a Qat

don't forget ↗
the sloppy parts!!!

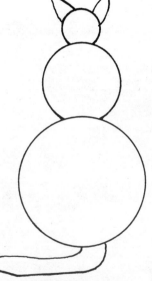

1. DRAW CIRCLE

2. DRAW TWO MORE CIRCLES

3. ADD EARS AND TAIL

4. TURN DRAWING AROUND AND THERE'S YOUR QAT!

Fig 1.

MAN LYING TO A CAT

PURSEY CAT

Feeding Ham to Cats

SUPERSTITIONS · KICK A CAT AND YOU'LL LOSE YOUR HAT.

KITTY HAWK

A Dreaded Hamwort

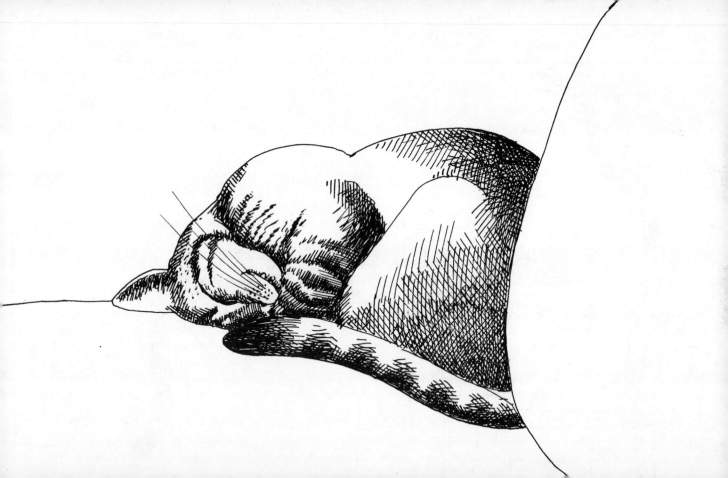

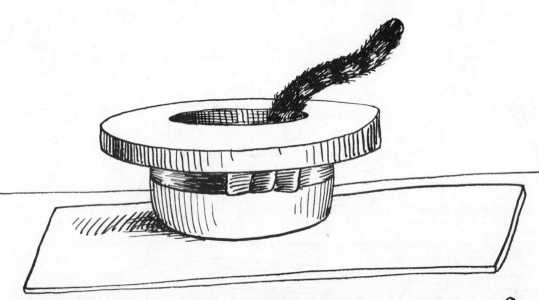

Cat in Fat Hat on Mat

Nit & the Ham Tree

Sleight of Paw

SUPERSTITIONS

KICK A CAT AND YOUR LEG WILL CRACK

FAT FUZZY FELLOW

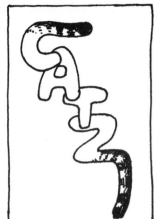

.... QUICK AS A WINK,
THE SLY CAT HAD EATEN
MONROE'S CHEESE SANDWICH.

Flot Cat in Slot Vat

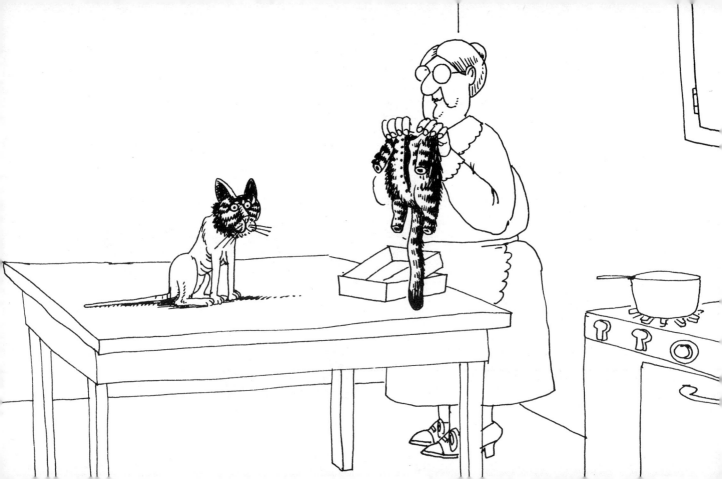

Nosechair Cat

...ITS GREAT TO BE HERE, FOLKS! I REALLY LOVE NEW YORK! ITS THE ONLY TOWN I KNOW WHERE THE MUGGERS AREN'T SAFE AT NIGHT! I GOT A HOTEL ROOM SO SMALL THE BEDBUGS WERE HUNCHBACKED! NO, BUT SERIOUSLY...

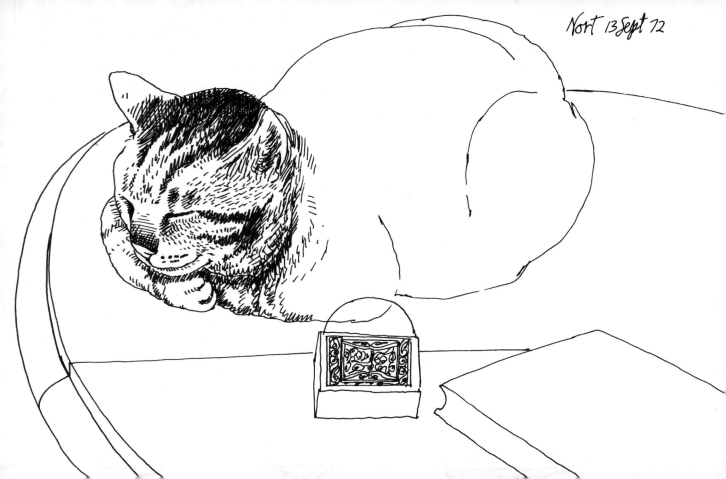

Nort 13 Sept 72

HOW TO TELL A CAT FROM A MEAT LOAF

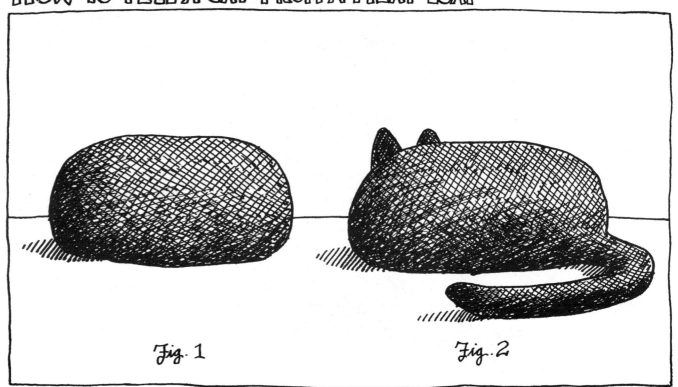

Fig. 1   Fig. 2

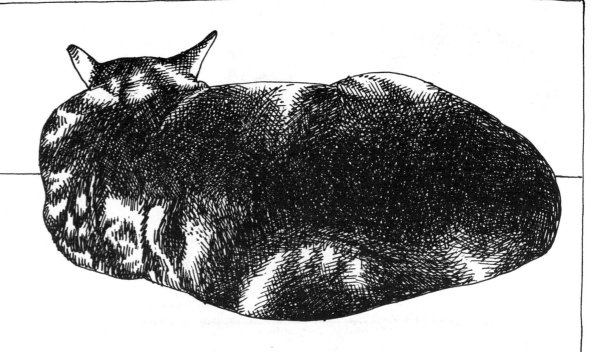

Nort NOV 72

Cats

Fig. 1

Fig. 2

Fig. 3

SMALL   MEDIUM   LARGE

Burton Rustle
20 Apr 74

Nit & Burt at the Same Time

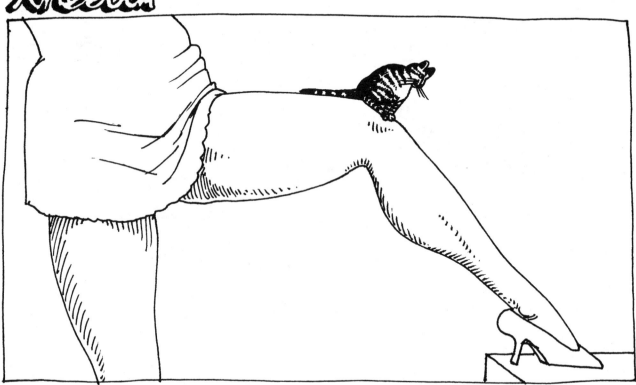

FAT NITTY

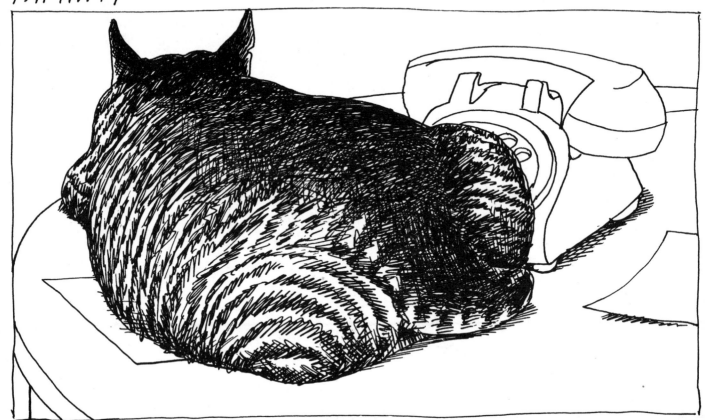

CATS CAN SEE THINGS WE CAN'T

SIAMESE WICKER CAT FIGHTING SUIT

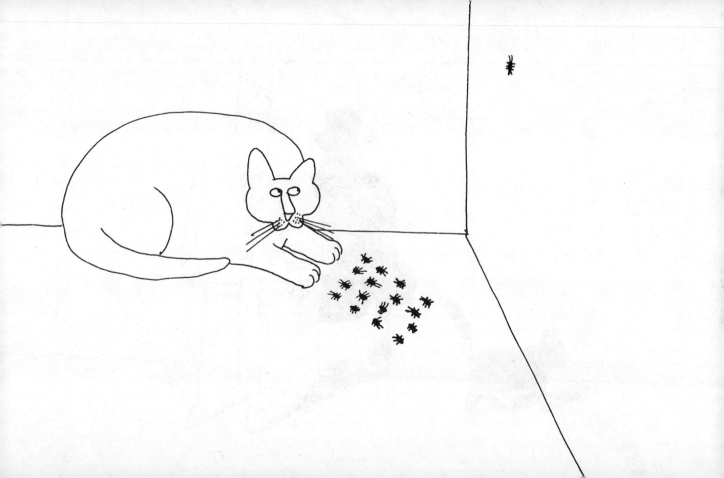

How to draw a Qat

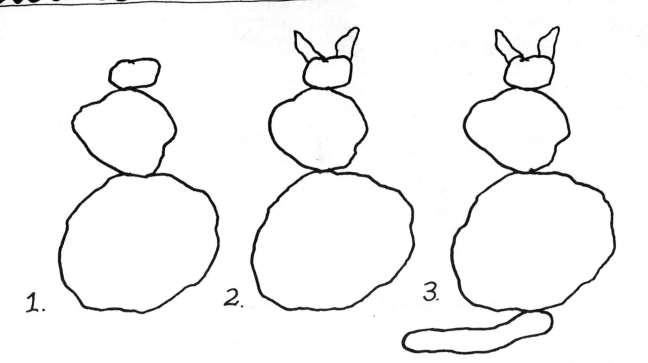

1.

2.

3.